coram
better chances for children since 1739

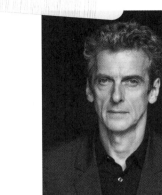

Thomas Coram was a visionary of his time. 350 years after he was born, this wonderful book tells the tale of his life and the origins of the Foundling Hospital, now simply known as Coram. It is a triumphant lesson in fighting for what is right, a philosophy at the very heart of the charity today as it continues to help vulnerable children and young people. The art of storytelling is vital in inspiring us all.

We hope that by reading Thomas Coram's story, you will be captivated by his courage and passion. While the history of the charity began hundreds of years ago, there are still children today who face difficulties in their lives and need Coram's help. Our hope is that by sharing in this story, you will see that when you fight for what is right, true and lasting change can happen.

So join me in reading this exciting, interesting and moving journey back to 1668 where it all began.

Peter Capaldi

My name is Thomas Coram. I was born in
Lyme Regis in Dorset in 1668 and have
always loved the sea and ships.

When I was 11 years old, I packed my
sea chest, boarded a trading ship and
sailed the high seas for five years!

It was not fun at the start, but then I got used to life on board and found my 'sea legs'.

What wondrous places and things I saw
during that time.

Returning home five years later, I became an 'apprentice'. I learned how to build ships like the ones on which I had sailed the seas.

Once my training was over, I set sail for America or the 'New World' as it was called. In such a growing country, there would surely be a need for ships!

After a lot of hard work I opened my own shipyard near Boston and made my name.

I played my part in creating the new States of America and worked to make sure that all children had the chance to learn, to read and write – girls as well as boys.

I returned to London with my wife, Eunice. I was horrified at what I saw on its streets – even babies abandoned because their mothers were so poor they could not care for them.

I decided that things must change and something must be done! So I began 'my darling project' to create a home for these 'Foundlings'.

At first no one would listen to me. But then I persuaded 21 noble ladies in the Court of Queen Caroline to sign a petition and present it to the King.

The King, George II, read it and after a lot of thought, he gave me his support. He signed a legal document called a 'Charter', which gave me permission to create my charity.

In 1739 the Foundling Hospital became a reality. Today it is just named after me – Coram!

The building opened in 1741 and
there were so many children that we
could not take them all.

Often mothers left tokens with their children hoping
that they could come back for them one day.

All the children had proper food, clothing and
a good education. If they became ill, they
were treated by the Queen's doctor.

The children had a new chance of life and were given new names. Some were named after my wife or me, others after famous people of the past like 'Julius Caesar'.

When they were old enough, the children left the
Foundling Hospital to start work. The boys often
joined the army as musicians, and the girls became
dressmakers or were servants in houses of rich people.

Many famous people gave their help. The painter
William Hogarth painted my portrait.

George Frederick Handel, the well-known composer, gave performances of his famous musical work called 'Messiah' to help the children and wrote a special Foundling Hospital anthem.

The writer Charles Dickens lived nearby. He helped mothers find places for their children at the Foundling Hospital. One of his characters in his book 'Little Dorrit' is called 'Tattycoram'.

A lot changed in the twentieth century. Children gained more equal chances, and our Foundling Hospital became Ashlyns School in Berkhamsted.

300 years after I started helping children, there was the United Nations Convention on the Rights of the Child.

Now I am buried in St Andrew's Church in Holborn and my work carries on. Coram continues to fight today for children in need of help, and makes sure children are always heard.

My friend Harold the Giraffe travels around the country with Coram Life Education. He visits schools to help children learn more about how to keep themselves safe.

Today you can visit my statue in London and hear my story in Brunswick Square. We will always be here to help children!

Helping you with words

Abandoned: Left alone without help

Anthem: A song of praise and loyalty

Apprentice: Someone training for work

Charter: A legal document giving the right to something

Convention: An agreement to make things happen

Foundling: An abandoned child found in need of help

Petition: A formal written request by many people

Sea Legs: An abililty to keep your balance on a boat and avoid being sea sick

Token: A mark or object which helps you remember or identify

Wondrous: Magical and special